JUL 1 4

SKYDIVING DOGS

by Meish Goldish

**Consultant: Mike Ritland, Navy SEAL Canine Trainer
Former Member of SEAL Team 3
Founder of the Warrior Dog Foundation**

BEARPORT
PUBLISHING

New York, New York

Credits

Cover and Title Page, © Central European News; Cover TR, © Kevin Carlile/DOD/Sipa Press/0910072019; Cover CR, © Keystone–France/Gamma–Keystone via Getty Images; Cover BR, © ZUMA Press, Inc./Alamy; TOC, © Courtesy of Skydive Townsville; 4, © Rex Features via AP Images; 5, © Rex Features via AP Images; 6, © Rex Features via AP Images; 7, © Rex Features via AP Images; 8, © Keystone–France/Gamma–Keystone via Getty Images; 9, © JOHN VIZCAINO/ Reuters/Corbis; 10, © Bettmann/Corbis/AP Images; 11, © Courtesy of IWM; 11TR, © Airborne Assault Museum; 12, © SWNS.com; 13L, © Airborne Assault Museum; 13R, © HANDOUT/KRT/Newscom; 14, © Terrence Spencer/Time Life Pictures/Getty Images; 15, © U.S. Air Force; 16, © Vince Vander Maarel /DOD/Sipa Press/0910072019; 17, © Kevin Carlile/DOD/Sipa Press/0910072019; 18, © Mike Ritland courtesy of ITS Tactical; 19, © Mike Ritland; 19TR, © U.S. Army photo by Kevin Carlile; 20, © HO/Reuters/Corbis; 21, © AP Photo/Saurabh Das; 22, © Central European News; 22–23, © Europics/Newscom; 24, © Autumn Cruz/ZUMA Press/Corbis; 24BL, © U.S. Army Sgt. Jason Brace; 25, © ZUMA Press, Inc./Alamy; 26, © Evan Morgan/Newspix; 27, © Courtesy of Skydive Townsville; 28, © JIM SMITH/AFP/Getty Images; 29TL, © Erik Lam/Shutterstock; 29TR, © Eric Isselee/Shutterstock; 29BL, © iStockphoto/Thinkstock; 29BR, © Tracy Morgan.

Publisher: Kenn Goin
Senior Editor: Joyce Tavolacci
Creative Director: Spencer Brinker
Design: Dawn Beard Creative
Photo Researcher: Picture Perfect Professionals, LLC

Library of Congress Cataloging-in-Publication Data

Goldish, Meish, author.
  Skydiving dogs / by Meish Goldish.
    pages cm. — (Dog heroes)
  Audience: Ages 7–12.
  ISBN-13: 978-1-62724-087-1 (library binding)
  ISBN-10: 1-62724-087-X (library binding)
  1. Dogs—War use—Juvenile literature. 2. Dogs—Training—Juvenile literature. 3. Working dogs—Juvenile literature. 4. Skydiving—Juvenile literature. I. Title. II. Title: Sky diving dogs. III. Series: Dog heroes.
  UH100.G639 2014
  355.4'24—dc23

                                     2013037776

For more information, write to Bearport Publishing Company, Inc., 45 West 21st Street, Suite 3B, New York, New York 10010. Printed in the United States of America.

10 9 8 7 6 5 4 3 2 1

Table of Contents

A Daring Dive

In July 2013, a team of **paratroopers** glanced out the small windows of an airplane. Each soldier wore a special backpack with a parachute tucked inside. As the plane soared more than 1,000 feet (305 m) in the air, the soldiers lined up near a door in the side of the plane. Each paratrooper waited for his chance to jump out and **skydive** to the ground.

The paratroopers prepare to parachute from their plane.

The paratroopers are members of the Air Force of Colombia, a country in South America. The team is trained to swoop down from the skies to find bombs and battle **terrorists**.

One team member, **Officer** Jorge Herrera, however, was carrying more than just his parachute pack. He also had a furry, four-legged passenger strapped to his chest. Jany, a specially trained **military** dog, was about to leap out of the aircraft with Officer Herrera!

Officer Jorge Herrera and Jany, a type of dog called a Belgian Malinois (mal-uhn-WAH), get ready to leap.

Parachuting to Work

When the airplane reached the **drop zone**, Officer Herrera leaped out with Jany. The dog had skydived dozens of times before and showed no sign of fear. After **free-falling** for a few seconds, Officer Herrara tugged a **rip cord** to open their parachute. Then the dog and her **handler** safely floated to the ground.

Officer Herrera and Jany seconds before jumping

Belgian Malinois, like Jany, are often used by military forces. They are smart, tough, and can smell up to 100 times better than a person!

After landing, Jany quickly got to work. She is trained to use her keen sense of smell to find hidden **explosives** and terrorists carrying bombs or other weapons. Jany's superb skydiving and sniffing skills make her one of the most valued members of the team!

After jumping out of the plane, Jany and Officer Herrera sail through the air.

Early Jumpers

Jany isn't the first military dog to skydive. **Canines** were first trained to parachute during World War II (1939–1945) in England. At that time, they were taught to jump without a human partner. The British military trained the dogs to skydive so that they could get to battle areas that had few roads and were hard to reach by land. After the dogs safely jumped out of planes, they could then help soldiers on the ground—but how?

Most of the military dogs trained by the British during World War II were German shepherds, such as the one shown here.

During World War II, the United States military also trained skydiving dogs. The dogs were used to find victims injured in plane crashes and drag them to safety.

Military dogs are trained to squeeze into tight spaces and use their noses to sniff out hidden bombs. They can also use their powerful sense of smell to **detect** enemy soldiers waiting in **ambush**. Because canines work quickly and quietly, they can also approach enemy targets without getting noticed.

Today, the U.S. military still uses German shepherds. This one is sniffing for explosives.

Learning to Leap

During World War II, dogs flew into battle areas to serve as the "eyes and ears" of soldiers on the ground. Who taught these military dogs to safely jump out of airplanes on their own? Ken Bailey, a British officer, was given the difficult task. The brave canines he trained became known as **paradogs**.

A soldier adjusts a paradog's parachute.

Before attempting a practice jump with the dogs, Officer Bailey made sure they were hungry. He hid tasty pieces of meat in his pocket so the dogs would follow him when he leaped out of the plane. When Officer Bailey brought a dog named Reena on a plane to skydive for the first time, he said, "I called out and she immediately turned in my direction and wagged her tail." After Reena and Officer Bailey each jumped out of the plane, they landed safely on the ground. Officer Bailey saw that Reena was "completely relaxed" and rewarded her with a meaty treat!

Officer Ken Bailey

Each of Officer Bailey's paradogs wore a parachute that opened automatically after the dog leaped from the plane.

A Hero Named Bing

One of the paradogs trained by Officer Bailey was a canine named Bing. Bing was one of the first dogs in the military to parachute behind enemy lines. "You'd see Bing . . . falling to Earth with . . . forepaws up and rear legs down, just as trained—ears flapping in the wind," said one former soldier. Bing showed great bravery in action. Once, he even leaped from an airplane while it was being hit by gunfire.

**Bing, the parachuting
canine soldier**

On the ground, Bing sniffed around for enemy soldiers. If he sensed danger, he would freeze and point his nose at where the trouble was. Bing watched over British troops even as they slept. Throughout the war, the brave dog saved the lives of hundreds of soldiers from enemy attacks.

Bing was awarded the Dickin Medal in 1947.

The Dickin Medal is a British award that honors the work of animals in war.

Bing receiving the Dickin Medal with his original owner, Betty Fetch

Reaching New Heights

After World War II, military groups continued to train dogs to skydive. Over time, however, the challenge for the dogs grew more difficult. The original British paradogs had jumped from less than one mile (1.6 km) above Earth's surface. Decades later, military dogs were being taught to skydive from much greater heights. Why was this necessary?

A U.S. Army parachuting dog in the 1960s

When paratroopers jump from high **altitudes**, it is easier for planes and soldiers to approach enemy territory without being seen. As a result, in the 1960s, U.S. Air Force paratroopers began jumping from heights of 35,000 feet (10,668 m)—nearly seven miles (11 km) above Earth. Jumping from these new heights, however, meant that skydiving dogs would need to be trained in a new way.

U.S. Air Force Colonel Joseph W. Kittinger II skydiving from high above the clouds

In 1960, Colonel Joseph W. Kittinger II of the U.S. Air Force set a record by making a high-altitude jump from 19.5 miles (31 km) above the ground!

Parachute Partners

Jumping from high above Earth, dogs could no longer parachute **solo**. Why? At altitudes of four miles (6.4 km) or higher, skydivers free-fall for several miles before opening their chutes. They do this in order to reach the ground more quickly. A dog can't open a parachute on its own, so the canine must ride with a human who can pull the rip cord.

Sometimes, two skydivers and a dog jump together as a team. Skydivers free-fall at a speed of about 125 miles per hour (201 kph).

Dogs also need parachute partners for another reason. After their chutes open, high-altitude skydivers guide themselves toward a target on the ground. To do this, they steer by pulling special straps on their parachute. Since a dog can't steer a chute, a paratrooper must do so.

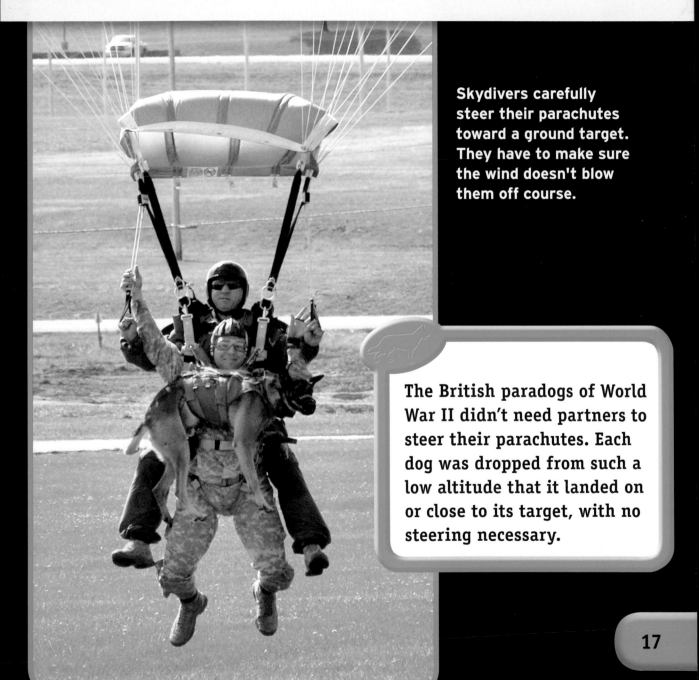

Skydivers carefully steer their parachutes toward a ground target. They have to make sure the wind doesn't blow them off course.

The British paradogs of World War II didn't need partners to steer their parachutes. Each dog was dropped from such a low altitude that it landed on or close to its target, with no steering necessary.

The Right Kind of Dog

Even with a human partner, skydiving can be a scary experience for some dogs. Mike Ritland is a dog trainer for the U.S. **Navy SEALs**. He says that very few canines make good skydivers. That's because most dogs have an **instinct** to keep all four paws on the ground—not in the air!

Mike Ritland trains military dogs on his ranch in Texas.

Mike Ritland was a U.S. Navy SEAL for 12 years before he began to train dogs for the military.

To see if a dog will make a good jumper, Mike first gets it used to being in high places, such as riding in a plane. Then, after the dog is comfortable in the air, he puts the canine in a **harness** and hangs it out of a helicopter. If the dog relaxes in the air, Mike feels it will probably make a good skydiver. If it is tense, he tries another dog. Mike looks for dogs that stay calm in the air but are tough on the ground. He calls those rare dogs "the one percent of the one percent."

A dog wearing a skydiving harness

Mike teaches dogs to feel comfortable both in the air and in the water.

Special Equipment

To succeed as skydivers, dogs need more than just the right personality. They also need the right equipment. When jumping from altitudes greater than 22,000 feet (6,706 m), both human and dog skydivers must wear oxygen masks. Why? At high altitudes, there is not enough oxygen in the air. The masks provide the extra oxygen skydivers need to breathe. Without it, the divers would become dizzy and pass out.

At high altitudes, both people and dogs need oxygen masks so they can breathe.

Once on the ground, U.S. Navy SEAL dogs use other special equipment. Some dogs have tiny cameras strapped to their backs and travel ahead of the SEALs to search for enemy troops. The cameras send the pictures back to the SEALs, showing them enemy locations. The dogs also wear special glasses that allow them to see in the dark.

Many military working dogs wear bulletproof vests in case they are caught in a gun battle while on the job.

A dog wearing a bulletproof vest

Working Together

The **armed forces** of countries all over the world use skydiving dogs. In 2010, troops and dogs from 14 countries came together to take part in military training **exercises** in Norway. The goal of the exercises was to prepare the soldiers and dogs to find and fight terrorists. In one exercise, Austrian paratroopers skydived with Belgian shepherds from a height of 10,000 feet (3,048 m).

Skydiving dogs often wear a muzzle over their nose and mouth. This protects their snout from hitting the ground upon landing.

The soldiers were impressed by the way the dogs stayed calm during the flights. One handler praised his canine partner, saying, "He has a much cooler head than most **recruits**." Another handler explained why dogs stay calm in the air. "They don't **perceive** height difference the same way humans do. . . . They're more likely to be bothered by the roar of the engines, but once we're on the way down . . . they just enjoy the view."

A skydiving dog and his handler in Norway

Since 2001, four-legged skydivers have helped American and British soldiers fight the **War on Terror.**

Jumping for Joy

Not all skydiving dogs serve in the military. Some dogs jump just for fun. In 2003, Otis the pug began leaping with his skydiving owner, Will DaSilva. Otis made his first jump when he was just one year old. Like other skydiving dogs, Otis wore goggles called doggles to protect his eyes. He also wore a harness that was specially made for his short, stocky body.

Will and Otis

A dog wearing doggles

Did Otis like to skydive? He seemed to love it, according to Will. His owner also noticed that the dog would get excited and then nervous right before the jump. "Once he's out, though, he's just having a ball." Otis was so relaxed before skydiving that he often fell asleep on the airplane before the jump!

Otis made a total of 65 jumps with Will.

During one dive, Will and Otis jumped from a height of about 3,000 feet (914 m).

Birthday Flight

Like Otis, Crasha is a dog that first skydived at the age of one. In fact, the jump was the miniature fox terrier's birthday present from her owner, Alan Moss, a skydiving instructor in Australia. Alan believed that Crasha would enjoy the jump because she had spent so much time riding with him in airplanes. "She is used to the heights," Alan explained.

Alan tosses Crasha into the air to get her used to the feeling of falling.

The pair jumped from an altitude of about 11,800 feet (3,597 m). After skydiving together and landing safely on a beach, Alan said that their jump "went great." How many more dogs might skydive in the future? Whether they're fighting terrorists or diving just for fun, the sky's the limit!

Alan and Crasha skydiving together

Alan was so pleased with Crasha's skydive that he said it would be hard to find a better present for the dog's second birthday.

Just the Facts

- U.S. military dogs and their handlers perform two kinds of high-altitude jumps. In a high-altitude low-opening (HALO) jump, the skydivers free-fall for several minutes before they open the parachute. In a high-altitude high-opening (HAHO) jump, the chute is opened just seconds after the divers leap from the airplane. HAHO skydivers may glide up to 40 miles (64 km) across the sky before landing.

- Hooch, a cross between a cattle dog and a King Charles spaniel, is believed to be the only dog ever to skydive and scuba dive. She had to quit jumping and diving, however, after she fell out of bed and broke her leg!

Any kind of dog can learn to skydive. Here are several dog breeds featured in this book.

Belgian Malinois

German shepherd

Pug

Miniature fox terrier

altitudes (AL-tuh-toods) the heights of things above the ground

ambush (AM-bush) to attack from a hidden position

armed forces (ARMD FORSS-iz) the military groups a country uses to protect itself

canines (KAY-nyenz) members of the dog family

detect (di-TEKT) to notice or discover something

drop zone (DROP ZOHN) the area where skydivers try to land

exercises (EK-sur-*syez*-iz) activities that are used for training

explosives (ek-SPLOH-sivz) things that can blow up, such as bombs

free-falling (FREE-FAWL-ing) dropping through the air before opening a parachute

handler (HAND-lur) a person who trains and works with an animal

harness (HAR-niss) a set of straps around an animal's chest

instinct (IN-stingkt) behavior that is natural rather than learned

military (MIL-uh-*ter*-ee) having to do with the armed forces of a country

Navy SEALs (NAY-vee SEELZ) a group of soldiers in the U.S. Navy who are specially trained to fight at sea, in the air, and on land

officer (AWF-uh-sur) a person in the military who leads others

paradogs (PA-ruh-DAWGZ) military dogs that jump from planes during wartime

paratroopers (PA-ruh-*troo*-purz) soldiers who are trained to jump by parachute into battle

perceive (pur-SEEV) to use the senses to become aware of something

recruits (ri-KROOTS) people who have recently joined the military

rip cord (RIP kord) a cord used to open a parachute

skydive (SKYE-dive) to jump from an airplane and fall freely before opening a parachute

solo (SOH-loh) done by oneself

terrorists (TER-ur-ists) individuals or groups that use violence and terror to get what they want

War on Terror (WOR ON TER-ur) a worldwide military fight against terrorists led by the United States and Great Britain after the attacks on the United States on September 11, 2001

Bibliography

Goodavage, Maria. *Soldier Dogs: The Untold Story of America's Canine Heroes.* New York: Dutton (2012).

Ritland, Mike, and Gary Brozek. *Trident K9 Warriors: My Tale from the Training Ground to the Battlefield with Elite Navy SEAL Canines.* New York: St. Martin's Press (2013).

Rogak, Lisa. *The Dogs of War: The Courage, Love, and Loyalty of Military Working Dogs.* New York: St. Martin's Press (2011).

Read More

Boyd, Gil. *The Amazing Adventures of Bing the Parachuting Dog.* Somersham, England: Impression Publishing (2012).

Goldish, Meish. *Soldiers' Dogs (Dog Heroes).* New York: Bearport (2013).

Goldish, Meish. *War Dogs (America's Animal Soldiers).* New York: Bearport (2012).

Learn More Online

Visit these Web sites to learn more about skydiving dogs:

www.nypost.com/p/news/opinion/opedcolumnists/zero_bark_thirty_5Q5vfvWqrin9A4fqbOLBUO

www.paradata.org.uk/content/para-dogs

http://www.telegraph.co.uk/history/world-war-two/10211307/Paradogs-lured-with-meat-out-of-aircraft-behind-enemy-lines-in-WWII.html

www.trikos.com

Index

About the Author

Meish Goldish has written more than 200 books for children. His book *Disabled Dogs* was a Junior Library Guild Selection in 2013. He lives in Brooklyn, New York.

RICHMOND HEIGHTS